TERM PAPERS
STEP BY STEP
Planning, Research, and Writing

by Clark Stevens

J. Weston Walch, Publisher
Portland, Maine

REPRODUCTION OF BLACKLINE MASTERS

These blackline masters are designed for individual student use and intended for reproduction by dry copier, liquid duplicating machine, or other means.

J. Weston Walch, Publisher, therefore transfers limited reproduction rights to the purchaser of these masters at the time of sale. These rights are granted only to a single classroom teacher, whether that teacher is the purchaser or the employee of a purchasing agent such as a school district. The masters may be reproduced in quantities sufficient for individual use by students under that teacher's direct classroom supervision.

Reproduction of these masters for use by other teachers or students is expressly prohibited and constitutes a violation of United States Copyright Law.

1 2 3 4 5 6 7 8 9 10

ISBN 0-8251-1781-X

Copyright © 1991
J. Weston Walch, Publisher
P. O. Box 658 • Portland, Maine 04104-0658
Printed in the United States of America

Contents

To the Teacher .... *v*

Masters

I. Understanding Yourself and the Writing Process
1. What Makes Writing Term Papers Difficult?
2. Understanding the Writer's Facts of Life
3. Writer's Block I: Negative Self-Talk
4. Developing a Winning Writer's Attitude
5. Remembering to Relax

II. Getting Ready to Work
6. Writer's Block II: Working Against Your Best Work Style
7. Planning a Work Environment That Works for You
8. Budgeting Time for the Tasks Ahead
9. Making the Best Use of a Computer
10. Getting Yourself in a Writing Mood
11. Writer's Block III: Procrastination
12. Strategies for Overcoming Procrastination

III. Starting the Assignment
13. Making Sure You Understand Your Assignment Completely
14. Shaping the Assignment to Fit Your Interests
15. Writer's Block IV: Blocked for Starting Ideas
16. Brainstorming to Generate Ideas
17. Freewriting to Get a Flow Going
18. Clustering to Develop and Focus Your Ideas
19. Tapping Your Imagination for Fresh Points of View
20. Drawing on Your Nonverbal Mind
21. Taking Advantage of Incubation Time
22. Working Out a Preliminary Plan for Your Paper

IV. Tackling Research
23. Writer's Block V: Getting Bogged Down in Research
24. Exploring Available Resources
25. Previewing Sources Before Plunging In

26. Some Important Tips on Note-Taking
27. Understanding and Avoiding Plagiarism
28. Looking Ahead to Your Paper's Footnotes or Endnotes
29. Looking Ahead to Your Paper's Bibliography

V. Organizing Your Argument
30. Writers Block VI: Trying to Avoid Making an Outline
31. Determining the Main Idea of Your Argument
32. Developing Your Argument with Subarguments
33. Choosing the Best Structure for Your Argument
34. Supporting Your Argument with Evidence
35. Anticipating Counterarguments

VI. Writing the First Draft
36. Writer's Block VII: Struggling with Perfectionism
37. Some Important Tips About Writing the First Draft
38. Tackling the Introduction
39. Building a Strong Conclusion
40. Drafting Paragraphs with Punch
41. Communicating Your Argument with Clear Transitions

VII. Revising and Polishing Your Work
42. Some Important Tips About Revising
43. Double-Checking Your Organization
44. Checklist for Avoiding Common Argument Fallacies
45. Checklist for Eliminating Word Clutter
46. Checklist for Developing a More Forceful Style
47. Checklist for Eliminating Sexist Language
48. Checklist for Avoiding the Most Common Grammar Errors
49. Checklist for Avoiding the Most Common Punctuation Errors
50. Writer's Block VIII: Skipping the Final Step—Proofreading

To the Teacher

When you stop to think about it, writing a good term paper is a surprisingly complex task that requires a wide variety of skills, both mechanical and psychological. Is it any wonder that students encounter difficulties?

For many, the move from writing "reports" to more demanding "term papers" or "research papers" is a big step. The expectations are suddenly higher, and the whole process requires much greater concentration and commitment. It's easy to get bogged down, confused, bored, discouraged, and very frustrated along the way.

Textbooks traditionally focus on the mechanics of a successful term paper: note-taking, outlines, footnotes and bibliography, grammar and punctuation, and so on. These formal elements are important and certainly need to be mastered.

But writing is also an intensely personal act that draws on each student writer's individual interests and feelings. The process is greatly affected by students' attitudes toward the task and toward themselves as writers. For each of them, writing at times can become a lonely—and sometimes terrifyingly isolated—task. This subjective side of the writing process often receives far less discussion in writing texts than the mechanics.

The Aims of These Materials

First and foremost, these materials are intended to show student writers that they are not *alone* in facing the many difficulties of writing term papers. These reproducible sheets have been written in a supportive, empathetic tone that recognizes that good writing is never easy.

Equally important, these materials have been designed to focus specifically on the most important problem areas where students experience difficulties. Very often writing texts bombard writers with too much "advice" to absorb all at once. Students get so overwhelmed in a mass of rules that the human element gets lost entirely.

These materials constantly reinforce the idea that successful research paper writing results from following a step-by-step process that takes *time*. This approach breaks up this process into smaller, isolated steps.

Assuming students have had previous experience with the basics of report writing, these materials cover the important mechanics related specifically to the stages of term-paper writing: idea-generating strategies, research skills, outlining, drafting, and revising. Equally important, these materials also address the psychological realities of writing—setting positive attitudes, assessing work styles, overcoming various writing blocks, and using assorted techniques to get students to engage themselves fully—from the heart—in their writing task.

Format

The packet contains 50 reproducible student sheets. Each sheet focuses on a different writing problem faced by average students writing term-paper assignments at the upper high school level. The sheets have been written in an easy-to-understand style that emphasizes practical solutions to common problems.

Each sheet begins with an "Ideas to Think About" section, which presents introductory ideas about the target problem. The following "Techniques to Try" section then offers a range of *specific* strategies for handling the problem discussed.

The sheets are organized in a chronological sequence that follows the step-by-step process of writing a typical student research paper—from getting ready to work to proofreading the final product.

Suggestions for Using These Sheets

These materials have been designed for flexible use to fit your specific needs. They can be used selectively to address specific student problems, or used in sequence as a complete research paper writing course for the entire class. They can be used to reinforce other writing texts or used on their own as an independent research paper writing unit.

We hope you will find these sheets useful as a springboard for discussion in your classroom about what specific writing problems—mechanical *and* psychological—*your* students are facing in their research paper writing.

Since so much of writing success draws on the self-esteem of student writers themselves (how they feel about the task and about their abilities to complete the task), the psychological climate that *you*, the teacher, set is key to your students' success. Let students know you recognize that writing is not easy, that you expect them to run into stumbling blocks. (You could even share stories of your own struggles with writing, past or present.)

A Final Note

In sum, this set of reproducible masters has been designed to help you help your students to change the research paper assignment from a painful chore into a more personally rewarding—and even enjoyable—process.

Good luck!

Name: _____

WHAT MAKES WRITING TERM PAPERS DIFFICULT?

Ideas to Think About

Who Says Writing Term Papers Is Easy?

Students experience a wide range of problems with writing research papers. Do any of these comments sound like *you*?

- "Writing makes me anxious. No matter how hard I try, I always get blocked as soon as I sit down to face that blank page."
- "Writing research papers involves too much detail work—I'm not that organized."
- "The hardest part for me is getting started. I always put off writing until the very last minute."
- "I'm such a perfectionist, I *hate* everything I write the minute I get it on paper."
- "I get killed on grammar and punctuation. My papers come back with so much red ink I can't read what I originally wrote."
- "It's all so boring and irrelevant. What does writing term papers have to do with real life anyway?"

Writing Term Papers Draws on Many Skills

If you experience writing problems, take courage in realizing that you are not alone. Writing a research paper draws on a complex combination of many different skills.

Some skills involve writing mechanics—taking notes, making outlines, following rules of grammar and punctuation, and so on. Other skills are in the area of personal self-management—how you motivate and organize yourself to get the job done.

Techniques to Try

1. What Makes Writing Term Papers Difficult for You?

Review the student comments listed above. Then take a few minutes to list here all *your* complaints about writing research papers. (Be complete—try to list as many as you can think of.)

2. Do You Actually Enjoy Any Parts of the Research Writing Process?

Now take a moment to think about those aspects of research writing that you actually like—or at least don't find to be a problem for you. (Example: *"I like the research stage when I can search out answers to my questions about my topic."*) List them here.

3. Share Your Answers to Questions #1 and #2 with Other Members of Your Class

How many of your problems are also problems for others? Do others share the same strengths as you?

© 1991 J. Weston Walch, Publisher

Name: _____

UNDERSTANDING THE WRITER'S FACTS OF LIFE

Ideas to Think About

What Are the Writer's Facts of Life?

No matter what project they are working on, good writers all agree on certain basic "facts of life" about how to achieve effective writing:

- Good writing takes time. It *can't* be rushed.
- Good writing is written in stages. It benefits from being left to sit in periods throughout the writing process.
- Good writing has something to say. The quality of its content is a direct result of the time and effort invested in developing its ideas.
- Good writing is organized logically.
- Good writing is clearly expressed, most often as a result of careful revision.
- Good writing results from effective "self-management"—such as budgeting time and working to get the most out of work sessions.
- Good writing depends on maintaining positive attitudes about the project and about *yourself* as a writer.
- Good writing depends on knowing how to handle negative emotions when you meet with frustrations along the way.

Techniques to Try

1. **How Healthy Are *Your* Writing Habits?**

    Review "The Writer's Facts of Life" above. Put a + in front of each fact that you already observe in your writing habits.

2. **Where Could You Improve Your Writing Habits?**

    Read through the list again and circle those facts that you do not presently follow in your writing work habits.

3. **Target Your Most Important Problem Areas**

    List the three *biggest* problem areas that you recognize you need to work further on:

a.

b.

c.

Name: _____

Writer's Block I: Negative Self-Talk

Ideas to Think About

Your Attitude Can Make All the Difference

A great deal of successful writing is a mind game. As in many other activities in your life, the negative attitudes you hold about your writing can sabotage your potential success.

Negative Self-Talk Undermines Your Writing Efforts

What you say and think about yourself as a writer influences how you write to a much greater extent than you probably realize.

Do any of these comments sound like the way *you* talk about yourself as a writer?

- "Good writers are born that way! Either you have it or you don't."
- "My teacher already knows that I can't write—what's the use?"
- "I'm good at math. I'm not a word person; I'm a numbers person."
- "Me write? Forget it! I never could and I never will!"

Negative Attitudes Sabotage Your Writing in Other Ways, Too

Students who do not feel confident about their writing often fall into the bad habit of reminding themselves about how they have "failed" in the past, rather than concentrating on how to improve their writing skills in the task ahead.

If they *do* decide to make a new start, these students often set themselves up with unrealistic expectations about what they should be able to accomplish or how fast they should be able to improve. And they also discourage themselves by constantly comparing themselves with better writers.

Techniques to Try

1. Do You Sabotage Your Writing Confidence with Bad Habits?

Take a moment to think about how you may be unnecessarily undermining your self-confidence as a writer:

- Do you allow yourself to be discouraged by dwelling on past "failures"?
- Do you discourage yourself by constantly comparing yourself with better writers?
- Do you set yourself up with unrealistic expectations about what you should be able to accomplish?

2. Listen to Your Self-Talk About Writing

When you are involved in a writing project, be attentive to any negative messages you may be sending to yourself when you are anxious, frustrated, tired, or discouraged.

a. What negative messages do you say to *yourself* about your writing? Write them here.

b. What negative messages do you say to *others* about your writing? Write them here.

Name: _____

DEVELOPING A WINNING WRITER'S ATTITUDE

Ideas to Think About

Build Your Self-Confidence for Success

Don't set yourself up to make your worst predictions come true. You can program yourself to get the **best** out of yourself just by changing the way you think—and talk—about your writing.

Replace Negative Self-Talk with Positive Messages

Don't be so hard on yourself! Replacing negative thinking with *positive* messages will quickly boost your self-confidence and give you more energy for working. It will also open up your receptivity to fresh ideas and outlooks and generally inspire you really to do your best.

Set Realistic, Achievable Goals for Writing Well

Being positive about your writing, however, does *not* mean setting wildly unrealistic expectations for yourself. You wouldn't expect to learn to play the guitar or become a champion swimmer overnight, so don't expect overnight miracles with your writing.

Set DO-able goals for yourself as a writer. And be ready to accept the inevitability of some struggle and frustration ahead.

Techniques to Try

1. **Program Yourself with Positive Messages About Your Writing**

    Review your negative self-talk messages from Sheet 3. Then try to write positive statements to replace your three most common negative self-talk messages. (Example: *"This paper is really going to be boring"* could become *"Since I want to improve my writing, I'm going to look for ways to make this project interesting to me."*)

    a.

    b.

    c.

2. **Start Each Paper Fresh!**

    Start with a clean slate when you begin each new writing project. Don't let thoughts about past "failures" sabotage you.

    Take the time you need to understand how you might learn from problems that you have encountered in the past—then let yourself off the hook.

3. **Don't Overburden Yourself with Unrealistic Expectations**

    In your heart, you know that you probably won't be able to conquer *all* your writing goals in one paper, no matter how hard you try.

    Think about what specific, attainable goals you might set for your new writing project. (Example: *"Working on organizing my ideas better. . . . Making sure I leave time for final revising and proofreading."*)

Name: _____

REMEMBERING TO RELAX

Ideas to Think About

Relaxed Writers Write Best

It's tempting to believe that you can force yourself to write well, no matter how tired or stressed you feel. But don't kid yourself—your mind and body are intimately involved in all stages of the writing process.

Tension in Your Mind or Body Works Against Writing Success

Tension has the opposite effect of relaxation on your mind and body. When you are anxious or tired, your muscles tighten and the energy you need to write at your best becomes blocked.

Good writing comes from good energy. When your body is tired from stress or lack of sleep, you cannot work at your best.

Relaxation Is Important to Good Writing

Getting yourself in a relaxed and rested state of mind can help at *all* stages of the writing process:

1. Getting you motivated to get started.

2. Keeping you supplied with fresh ideas as you plan your approach in the early stages of your paper.

3. Providing you with the energy to see your paper through the drafting and revision stages so that it ends up being the best you can write.

Techniques to Try

1. Make Relaxation a Part of *Your* Writing Process

What strategies do you already use to be sure you bring a relaxed mind and body to your writing tasks? Check them off here. What more can you do? Make the strategies you haven't checked off part of your routine. Then check them off too.

- Do you make sure to bring fresh energy to your writing by getting adequate sleep and rest?

- Do you take time out every day to help beat stress by getting regular exercise?

- Do you eat regular nutritious meals to give your body the fuel it needs to work at its best?

- Do you balance periods of work with time off to recharge your energies—such as spending time with friends and enjoying hobbies?

2. Tense? Try This Quick Technique for Instant Relaxation

Let go of tension with progressive relaxation, one of many stress-beating methods available. This will help induce a relaxed state of mind to improve your writing.

a. Sit in a comfortable chair, or lie on the floor on your back. Close your eyes. Gently inhale and exhale a slow, deep breath.

b. Now, focus your attention on your right foot. Gently tense it for five seconds. (Do not overstrain.) Then release the tension totally. Does the foot feel more relaxed?

c. Slowly work up the right side of your body, repeating this tensing and releasing procedure. Focus progressively on your right calf, right thigh, right fist, right forearm, and right upper arm. Then repeat on your left side.

d. Finish by tensing and relaxing the muscles of your face.

Name: _____

Writer's Block II: Working Against Your Best Work Style

Ideas to Think About

The Same Working Methods Do Not Work for Every Writer

Because different writers have different personalities, they often require different strategies to produce their best writing. All writers need to learn how to develop work habits and methods that work for *them*.

How Do Writers Work Against Their Natural Work Styles?

By not being attentive to their own best work-style needs, writers can find themselves working against themselves in a number of ways:

- **Time Use.** (Example: *Leaving a project until the last minute, when the writers know they don't work well under pressure.*)

- **Task Management.** (Example: *Being forced to work sequentially, when the writers prefer to jump around, mixing many tasks at once.*)

- **Tools.** (Example: *Working exclusively on a computer, knowing that they would produce more efficiently by working off the screen part of the time.*)

Make the Effort to Develop Work Habits That Work for You

Sometimes it seems easier to stay with work habits that you know are not best for you, rather than to make the effort to try new methods.

But how YOU work best is the best way for you to work. Make sure your work habit choices really do work best to get the job done.

Techniques to Try

1. **How Do *You* Work Best?**

    What are the characteristics of your writing personality? Underline the descriptions that fit you.

    - Do you work best calmly over time? or under pressure?

    - Do you like to work on a project methodically, step by step? or on many tasks all at the same time?

    - How's your attention span? Do you do your work best immersed in a task for a long period of time? or with more frequent, shorter stabs at the task?

2. **In What Ways Do You Know That You Work *Against* Yourself?**

    List three of your present writing work habits that you know don't really fit your best writing personality. (Example: *"I get bored easily if I have to work at the same task for too long a period."*)

    a.

    b.

    c.

3. **What Changes Could You Make in Your Work Habits That Would Fit *Your* Writer's Nature Better?**

    Look at the poor writing work habits you've listed above. What specific changes could you make in your work style to fit your personality better? (Example: *"I could work on more than one task at a time to allow me to shift back and forth to keep from getting bored."*) List the changes on the back of this page.

Name: _____

Planning a Work Environment That Works for You

Ideas to Think About

Your Work Environment Can Make the Difference Between Success and Failure

All writers have at least some opportunity to shape the kind of work environment they work in. To the extent that you can, it makes sense to design a work environment that fits *your* writing style.

Find a Setting That Fits *Your* Personal Working Style

Writers really *are* different. What characteristics in the list below fit your work style best? Underline them.

- Working in solitude? or with other people around?
- Working in quiet? or with background noise (such as radio or TV)?
- Working in a closed, intimate space? or in an open space with lots of light?
- Working in a neat, clean space? or in a space with lots of comfortable clutter?

Guard Against Distractions

Some people, intentionally or unintentionally, set themselves up to have their work time disrupted by interruptions. Some common examples:

- Working near a phone that is likely to interrupt your work.
- Choosing a work setting (such as a library or fast-food restaurant) where you are likely to run into friends.
- Getting started without making certain that you have all materials that you need (supplies, research materials, etc.).

Techniques to Try

1. What Work Environment Fits *You* Best?

First, take a moment to fantasize your ideal work space. Let your imagination run free—but envision a space that would realistically work to help you write at your best! (Example: *A treehouse with superfine stereo system and refrigerator stocked with nonstop cola!*) Describe your ideal workspace here:

Now, ask yourself which ideas you could actually incorporate in a work setting that is available to you now. (Example: *A desk by a window with a view of a tree and two cans of soda to drink during your work session.*)

2. Is Your Work Setting Distraction-Proof?

Do you sabotage yourself by choosing a work setting that sets you up to be a victim of distractions? List the distractions in your usual work setting(s):

What changes could you make to avoid distractions that get in the way of writing at your best? List the changes next to each distraction.

© 1991 J. Weston Walch, Publisher

Name: _____

BUDGETING TIME FOR THE TASKS AHEAD

Ideas to Think About

Good Writing Takes Time

Like many students, you have probably heard about "genius" writers who just sit down at the typewriter and spin out perfect *A* papers in one draft. Even if such stories are true, they are the exceptions to the rule. Face it: Writing takes *time*!

Schedule *More* Time Than You Think You'll Need!

Writing projects almost always take longer than you originally think. Plan ahead for setbacks such as false starts, unexpected interruptions, and running overtime.

Make Room for "Incubation Time"

Quality writing comes in stages with breaks for "incubation" in between—time to let your ideas develop on their own while *you* cool off. You need to schedule your work sessions with break time between to let ideas sit. This will allow you to return to your work with a fresh perspective.

Techniques to Try

1. Make a Time Budget Before You Start Working

Steps	*Estimated Time Needed*	*Actual Time Needed*
Understanding Assignment		
Brainstorming Ideas		
Making Preliminary Plan		
Research		
Drafting		
Revising Draft		
Final Polishing		
Proofreading		

2. Time Use Review

Keep track of your actual time expenditures at each stage to help you assess where you might need to budget *more* time on later papers. Also review your time use to determine where you might be able to work more efficiently and spend *less* time on your next paper.

Name: _____

MAKING THE BEST USE OF A COMPUTER

Ideas to Think About

The Computer Can Be a Powerful Writer's Tool

Without question, using a computer to write a term paper has *many* benefits. The computer's word-processing functions easily allow you to enter changes in your draft and then see it instantly reprinted—without having to retype the whole draft!

Also, spellchecker and other supplementary computer programs can help you to edit and proofread your final text.

But Be Aware of Computer Dangers, Too

It's easy to be excited by the computer's benefits. But you may overlook some of the *negative* effects that computer use can have on how you write: physical and mental fatigue.

- **Eyestrain.** Working for uninterrupted periods of time at a computer's monitor screen can induce eyestrain and headache.

- **Neck and Back Strain.** Working for uninterrupted periods of time in one sitting position can also cause neck and back strain due to poor posture.

- **Mental Fatigue.** Working closely for long periods with the computer can also put you into a kind of "hypnotic" mental state where you become far less efficient in your thinking patterns.

Don't Let the Computer Lure You into Editing Too Early

Yes, the computer makes editing easy—perhaps too easy. Don't let the computer's ease of revising induce you into polishing your word choices, sentences, or paragraphs *before* you've actually written a complete draft. Concentrate first on just getting a rough draft on paper. Edit and revise later.

Techniques to Try

1. Stay Aware of Your Computer Work Habits

Stay aware of the physical effects that your computer work habits are having on your body and mind:

Eyes. Does the balance of light from windows, overhead light, desk light, and monitor screen feel comfortable to you? Do you notice any glare on the monitor screen that should be corrected? When you work at the computer, do you keep your eyes at a comfortable distance from the screen?

Posture. When you work at the computer, do you keep your back straight and supported by the back of your chair?

2. Take Frequent Short Breaks

Because working at the computer is such an all-involving activity, it's easy to forget to keep aware of your body's needs. Give your eyes frequent "vacations" by frequently looking away from the screen. Eliminate body tension by reminding yourself to get up and stretch periodically.

3. When Possible, Work on Your Paper *Away* from the Computer

Don't let the computer screen hypnotize you and turn you into a writing zombie. Get away from the computer when you can: Write your first draft in longhand. Or print out your drafts and edit them on paper before entering changes on the computer.

Name: _____

GETTING YOURSELF IN A WRITING MOOD

Ideas to Think About

Pamper Yourself into a Writing Mood!

Writing, like all other activities that require effort, is work. It can be a lonely business. It's natural that few of us want to rush into it. You may have to work to get yourself into the writing mood.

Take Time to Warm Up Before a Writing Workout

Just as athletes need to warm up before an exercise workout, so writers need to use different strategies to get their brains in gear for a good writing session.

The personal routines that writers use to get themselves ready to write are called "readiness rituals." Some common examples include:

- Neatening the work space.
- Sharpening pencils.
- Preparing a favorite drink (coffee, tea, cola).
- Preparing a favorite snack.
- Activities to clear the mind (taking a walk, doing yoga).
- Playing favorite music.
- Changing into special "writing clothes" (wearing a favorite sweatshirt or cap).

Develop Your Own Personal Routine—and Stick to It

Once you've found effective strategies to get yourself into a writing mood and to make the writing session enjoyable, work them into your work routine every time.

Techniques to Try

1. How Do *You* Warm Up Before a Writing Workout?

What "readiness rituals" do you use now to get you in a writing mood? Which ones work best for you? Check them off in the list above.

What other warm-up strategies could you try? List them here.

2. Leave Unfinished Business to Begin Your Next Work Session

One effective warm-up strategy recommended by professional writers is to leave your previous work session with a simple *unfinished* task. Then you can begin your next session by completing this task to get you warmed up for more difficult writing work.

Name: _____

WRITER'S BLOCK III: PROCRASTINATION

Ideas to Think About

Real Procrastination Activities Ultimately Work Against You

Some stalling is actually a form of incubation. You really *are* working on the paper while you give yourself time to get ready.

But sometimes you find yourself choosing procrastination activities to avoid writing altogether. Such activities are seldom enjoyable in themselves because all you can focus on is *not* working on your writing!

Recognizing Procrastination Symptoms

Procrastination shows up in a wide variety of behaviors such as these:

- Keeping yourself active with other chores, such as cleaning your room or writing important letters.

- Making sure you work in a setting where it is likely that you will be distracted by phone calls, friends visiting, etc.

- Making many false starts at writing but then eventually allowing yourself to be distracted by another activity.

- Allowing yourself suddenly to get "sick" or injured to avoid writing.

Why Do Writers Procrastinate?

Writers procrastinate for many different reasons, some simple and some complex:

- They may feel no confidence in their own writing abilities and try to avoid the frustration of writing.

- They may feel bored with the assignment and can't make themselves get down to it.

- They may make such perfectionist demands on their writing, they can't live up to their own unrealistic expectations.

- They may not be able to concentrate on writing because of other distractions in their lives (such as personal, family, or school problems).

Techniques to Try

1. Identifying Your Own Procrastination Strategies

Identifying your own procrastination tendencies is a start to overcoming them. Review the list of procrastination symptoms above. What methods of procrastination do *you* most tend to choose? Check them off. Can you add other symptoms to the list?

2. Identifying Why You Procrastinate

Review the list above of reasons why writers procrastinate. What are some reasons that motivate *you* to procrastinate? Check them off. Can you add other motivations to the list?

Name: _____

STRATEGIES FOR OVERCOMING PROCRASTINATION

Ideas to Think About

Make the Decision—and Effort—to Change

Procrastination activities are ultimately a waste of your time. They aren't enjoyable in themselves, and they don't bring you any closer to getting the task done.

Keep Fighting the Procrastination Urge!

Overcoming the anxiety that leads to procrastination is not always easy. Changing your underlying attitudes and work habits will call for continued effort on your part. Don't give in to your old bad habits!

Techniques to Try

Procrastination-Beating Strategy #1: Don't Overestimate the Pain

Don't let your mind imagine the writing task in front of you to be *more* painful than it really is. Try changing the way you perceive the task. Face up to the realities of the problem rather than running away from exaggerated difficulties:

- Ask yourself, "What is it that's really bothering me about the task?" (Example: *"It's going to take too much time to write. . . . I think the topic is boring."*)

- Are your fears realistic? Are there ways you can change your thinking about the task that would reduce its painfulness? (Example: *"Maybe if I plan out a schedule, I will see how I can fit working on this paper into my schedule."*)

- Is there anything you can do to make these aspects actually less painful? (Example: *"Maybe I can talk to my teacher about modifying the topic to make it more interesting to me."*)

Strategy #2: Focus on Rewards That Make the Pain Worth It

Even if the task ahead really is as painful as you imagine, you can undercut your urge to procrastinate by focusing on the actual benefits of completing the task. Focus on: "What's really in this for *me*?"

What benefits will come to you from facing up to the project? (Example: *"Improving my grade in this course will allow me to make the honor roll. . . . Working on my writing skills will improve my writing for the student newspaper."*)

Strategy #3: Just Get Started!

Sometimes it's hard to motivate yourself by imagining benefits that seem so far away or intangible. But you know that sooner or later you're going to have to get it over with. In such cases, just making the effort to get started can save you from a lot of wasted procrastination time.

Contract with yourself to work for a specific amount of time without giving in to procrastination activities. See what happens.

Name: _____

MAKING SURE YOU UNDERSTAND YOUR ASSIGNMENT COMPLETELY

Ideas to Think About

Avoid Later Problems by Starting Off Right

By not taking time *now* to understand your assignment fully, you could end up investing a lot of time and effort writing a paper that does not meet the expectations of the assignment.

Be Clear About the Mechanics of the Assignment

Don't sabotage your efforts from the start. Take time to read your assignment very carefully.

- **Due Date(s).** When is the final paper due? Does your teacher want to see evidence of progress along the way, such as note cards, outlines, or early drafts?
- **Length (Number of Pages).** How long should the paper be? Is there a minimum and/or maximum page limit?
- **Use of Sources.** What kinds of sources are you expected to consult? How many sources are expected?
- **Format Expectations.** Footnotes or endnotes? Bibliography?

Understand the Key Words in Your Assignment

Research paper assignments often include *key words* that have precise meanings you need to understand. Here are a few important words, with their common meanings, that you should know.

Analyze: Break up into its component parts.

Classify: Group and arrange to emphasize relationships.

Compare and Contrast: Show how the items are both similar *and* different.

Define or **Identify:** How is *this* item distinguishable from others like it?

Evaluate: Weigh and judge; show the importance of this item in comparison with others like it.

Illustrate or **Exemplify:** Give examples to show that you understand the concept.

Techniques to Try

1. **Are You Sure About the Terms of Your Assignment?**

    Due date? Length? Use of sources? Format requirements?

2. **Are You Sure About *All* the Key Words in Your Assignment?**

    Read through the entire assignment and underline the key words.

    If there are any that you are unsure about, consult your dictionary or your teacher for clarification.

3. **Do You Still Have Questions About the Assignment?**

    Don't waste one minute working on an assignment that you do not completely understand! *Now* is the time to go to your teacher for further clarification.

Name: _____

SHAPING THE ASSIGNMENT TO FIT YOUR INTERESTS

Ideas to Think About

You Can't Write Well If You're Turned Off

If you let yourself be turned off by an assignment from the start, writing well at each stage along the way becomes *extra* difficult.

Writing well is hard enough when you're really interested in a subject. Invest the time *now* to design a paper that will really interest you.

If Your Assignment Offers Choices, Choose to Fit *Your* Interests

Many assignments have some flexibility built in. Teachers design them to be open-ended on purpose to encourage you to develop a topic that really interests *you*.

Look for every way you can to "own" your assignment—to shape it to fit your real interests.

The Best Writing Is Writing from the Heart

Look for ways to get *you* into your writing. Take advantage of choices offered to tailor your topic choice to follow *your* interests.

- What aspect of the assignment makes you most curious?
- Where do you stand on the issues involved in the assignment?
- What experiences have you read about or had in your own life that attract you to one aspect of the assignment?

Techniques to Try

1. Take Time to Explore *All* Your Options

Where does *your* assignment specifically allow you choices? What is the range of options allowed by each choice?

2. Evaluate Your Options

The choices that seem easiest may turn out in the end to be *more* difficult because they don't motivate you to get personally involved in the assignment.

Trust your heart. What choices seem as if they would make the project most interesting and fun for you?

3. Still Having Trouble Connecting with Your Assignment?

Connecting personally with your assignment is a very important stage in your paper's ultimate success. Don't move ahead until you have really found an approach that will motivate you to give your best to the project.

If you are still having trouble finding a direction, talk to your teacher.

Name: _____

WRITER'S BLOCK IV: BLOCKED FOR STARTING IDEAS

Ideas to Think About

Facing the Blank Page

You've chosen your topic and need to start generating some ideas about how to develop the assignment. . . . You're facing a blank page—and suddenly discover that you have *nothing* to say. . . .

The techniques below, and on the sheets that follow, describe a variety of powerful strategies to help you get past the frustrating blocks that nearly all writers experience in the idea-generating stage of writing projects.

Get Yourself Started by Setting Specific Goals

One common cause of "starter's writing block" is finding yourself faced with *too much* freedom. You panic because you just don't know where to start first.

An effective strategy for overcoming "blank-page-itis" is to look for ways to limit the task before you. By setting smaller and more specific goals for yourself, you can program your idea-generating brain with instructions that are clearer and easier to execute.

And Don't Give In to Your "Censor"

If you are like most writers, you must deal with your "censor"—a part of yourself that is critical of *all* your ideas and never thinks any of them is any good.

Because you judge your ideas too soon, you don't even give yourself a chance to get started before rushing in to evaluate whether your ideas will work or not. Since your "censor" is so critical, you often end up throwing out good ideas.

Techniques to Try

1. **Strategies for Overcoming "Blank-Page-Itis"**

    You don't have to let a blank page spook you when starting to generate ideas for your paper.

    a. **State Your Overall Goal.** In your mind, state to yourself your overall objective. (Example: *"I need to develop ideas for my research paper assignment about . . ."*)

    b. **Then Break Up the Task into Parts.** Don't try to work on everything at once. Set subtasks for yourself. (Example: *"What questions should my paper answer? What major points should it contain? What evidence should I include? What aspects are most interesting to me?"*)

    c. **Program Yourself with Specific Expectations.** Put headings on different sheets to program each of your idea-generating tasks. Set realistic expectations to limit each task. (Example: *Five Questions My Paper Should Answer; Three Aspects About This Project That Particularly Interest* Me.)

    d. **Now Begin to Complete Each Idea-Generating Task.**

2. **Strategies for Beating Your "Censor"**

    Some of your "censor's" negative attitudes may spring from past writing experiences that determine how you feel about yourself as a student and as a writer today. Others may be brought on by tension, fatigue, or stress.

    Before moving on to the idea-generating sheets that follow, reread Sheets 3 and 4 on attitude and Sheet 5 on relaxation.

Name: _____

BRAINSTORMING TO GENERATE IDEAS

Ideas to Think About

Develop an Open Attitude to New Ideas

Being open means being receptive to new ways of looking at things. You see new patterns and plans, and ways of organizing them.

A flexible attitude is essential. Don't judge your ideas too early. Don't throw away good ideas that might fit.

What Is Brainstorming?

Brainstorming is a technique of nonjudgmental list-making used to generate and multiply ideas. It encourages you to focus on just generating ideas rather than evaluating them.

How Does Brainstorming Work?

Write your starting "seed" idea at the top of a piece of paper. (Example: *The Effects of the Invention of Television*)

Then write down—in single words or short phrases—*every* idea that occurs to you. Do not evaluate any of your ideas. Just write them down.

If you pause in your flow of ideas, try not to stop. Encourage your mind to keep working as long as possible. Often the last ideas are the best!

When you truly can't think of any more ideas, look at your list. If you want to, choose one of your new ideas to be the seed idea for another brainstorming list.

Techniques to Try

Use Brainstorming to Multiply and Develop Ideas

Any idea can be the starting seed of a brainstorming session. You can use brainstorming to turn a starting seed idea into many ideas, using it to generate a list of other ideas like it. For example, you might brainstorm a list of possible questions that your paper should answer.

You can also use brainstorming to break up a single idea into its many parts. For example, you might brainstorm to divide your topic into possible subcategories to explore approaches for organizing your paper.

Either way, just remember to write down the ideas that come to you—without judging them. Be inventive! And keep brainstorming as long as you can, because the best ideas often come just when you think you're dry.

Name: _____

FREEWRITING TO GET A FLOW GOING

Ideas to Think About

Reaching Below the Surface

Often when students encounter blocks in generating ideas for a paper, they believe it's because they have nothing to say. But that's not true. Underneath the surface of your frustrations lies a nearly endless supply of fresh ideas that are uniquely yours! The main trick is to get to them.

What Is Freewriting?

Freewriting is a powerful technique that helps you break through writing blocks. It's a tool used by even experienced writers when they find themselves unable to express ideas.

How Does Freewriting Work?

At the top of a sheet of paper, write the name of your subject. (Example: *The Causes of the American Revolution*) Set a timer for 10 minutes.

Then, start writing—and keep writing—without taking your pencil off the paper. Don't stop to correct or change anything.

If you run out of ideas, *keep writing:* nonsense words (example: *"blah, blah, blah"*); phrases about the thoughts going through your head (example: *"This is never going to work"*); even doodling.

The important thing is not to stop. Within a short period of time, you'll find you have another idea to write.

When the timer stops, review the ideas you have generated. You can choose to continue for another 10-minute period of writing. *Or* you may choose to write one of your new ideas on the top of another sheet of paper to use as the seed for another freewriting period with a new focus.

Techniques to Try

1. Use Freewriting to Explore Possible Ideas for Your Paper

Often you have more ideas about a subject than you give yourself credit for. Freewriting is an excellent technique for mining thoughts that lie just below the surface of your conscious mind.

For example, say your mind has gone dry developing interesting directions for your paper. Write on the top of a blank sheet: "Of all the different approaches I could take toward this topic, I think the most interesting for me would be . . ." Then follow the rules of freewriting to explore what ideas may be lurking under the surface.

2. Use Freewriting to Explore Hidden Feelings, Too

When you find yourself blocked in your writing by feelings that are getting in the way, you can also use freewriting to help get those feelings more out in the open.

For example, to explore feelings that may be keeping you from developing ideas for your paper, write on a blank sheet: "I think I may be blocked right now because I'm feeling . . ." Then use freewriting to explore feelings that are bothering you.

Name: _____

CLUSTERING TO DEVELOP AND FOCUS YOUR IDEAS

Ideas to Think About

What Is Clustering?

Clustering is a specific brainstorming technique. Like freewriting, it is especially effective in helping you get below the surface of your thinking to discover fresh patterns of ideas and connections.

When to Use Clustering

Similar to brainstorming and freewriting, clustering can be used to help you generate ideas relating to a specific topic when you feel blocked.

Clustering can also help you find a useful focus when you have too many confusing ideas and are looking for a way to organize them.

A Method for Clustering

Draw a small circle in the middle of a blank sheet of paper.

Decide on a seed word or phrase for your cluster (example: *Shakespeare's London*). Write it in the circle.

Then, decide on a branch word or phrase, a category that relates to the seed word (example: *The Theaters*). Write it in a circle near the seed word and connect the two circles with a branch line.

Now you have two choices for branching. You can either add a second branch word off the seed word (example: *The Court*) or a new sprout word off the branch word (example: *Architecture*).

Keep the cluster growing by adding ideas off any circle, making new branches or subbranches. Let yourself be free. Write down anything that comes to mind—don't censor your ideas for appropriateness.

Fill the page if possible. Push yourself until you honestly can't flesh out the pattern any further.

Techniques to Try

1. Interpreting Your Cluster

When you have filled an entire page, or run out of ideas, stop writing and look over what you have written.

- What patterns of organization have emerged?
- What branch ideas most interest you? Do they suggest further avenues to explore?
- Do any new ideas surprise you? Do they suggest new directions to explore?

2. Developing Your Cluster

Often the best results from clustering come from second-generation clusters—a second cluster started from an idea generated in the first cluster.

To make a second-generation cluster, review your first cluster and choose a word or phrase that you would like to develop more. Make it the seed of a second, more focused cluster. Then repeat the clustering and interpreting processes already described.

Name: _____

TAPPING YOUR IMAGINATION FOR FRESH POINTS OF VIEW

Ideas to Think About

Tap into Your Imagination

Even after trying such techniques as brainstorming, freewriting, and clustering, some people still can't get a flow of ideas going.

If you are like many writers who need a different kind of push to get your juices flowing, your imagination can be the best writer's friend you've got.

Turn Your Thoughts into *Feelings*

Sometimes, by using your imagination, you can turn humdrum abstract thoughts into rich and lively ideas full of feeling and energy.

Some Techniques for Making Use of Your Imagination

Imagine Mental Pictures. Make your "seed" idea (example: *The French Revolution*) come alive in a scene in your imagination. Be sure to include elements to stimulate *all* your senses: sight, sound, smell, taste, and touch. When you have imagined a vital scene, then let the image generate ideas for you to write down.

Invent Imaginary Dialogues. Bring your seed idea (example: *The American Revolution*) to life by imagining yourself talking to a person somehow involved with the idea: a famous person from the past (example: *George Washington, King George*) or an imaginary participant or eyewitness (example: *a Minuteman, a Redcoat*).

Techniques to Try

1. Use Your Imagination to Bring Your Seed Idea to Life

To tap into the full power of your imagination, it's important to develop your imaginary scene with details from *all* your senses.

One useful technique is to imagine you are a news reporter right in the middle of the scene. Make a list of notes of every physical stimulus you experience—sights, sounds, tastes, smells, tactile sensations—and the ideas that occur to you with those stimuli.

2. Talk with Characters Involved with Your Seed Idea

Conduct an imaginary interview with someone, or a variety of people, involved with your seed idea.

Ask as many questions as you can: What was it like to be involved? What were their feelings about the experience? How do their feelings contrast with other figures who were involved? What aspects of the situation were most interesting from their point of view?

Name: _____

DRAWING ON YOUR NONVERBAL MIND

Ideas to Think About

Part of You Doesn't Think in Words

Writing makes use of your whole personality—the part of your brain that processes thoughts in words *and* the part of your brain that sees relationships between ideas in nonverbal patterns. Some researchers call these the left and right sides of the brain.

You Have Deeper Ideas Than You Think

Sometimes writers get blocked in generating ideas because they get too caught up in individual details. This makes it difficult to see the whole picture.

Your mind has more rich ideas and connections between ideas than you imagine. If you are relaxed and really interested in exploring, you may surprise yourself!

Some Techniques for Tapping the Nonverbal Side of Your Brain

Sometimes words *can* get in the way, especially if you are a person who tends to process information visually rather than verbally. If so, try some of these block-breaking techniques:

- **Listening to Music** while you write. The right choice of music for you (writers have different needs) can relax you and put you in a state of mind that encourages a flow of ideas.

- **Doodling.** Distract your censoring mind by taking a break from thinking. Let your pencil just move as it wants to and let your mind go.

- **Drawing, Diagramming, and Mapping.** If you are having a hard time developing your ideas in words, try drawing them. Visual thinking can help you get beyond blocks created by words and see your subject from fresh new perspectives.

Techniques to Try

1. Use Music to Inspire Your Creativity

Experiment with different musical styles as a background for your writing work sessions. What kind of music relaxes you? What kind of music puts you in a free, idea-generating frame of mind? Make sure not to choose music that is so stimulating that it distracts you—or so restful that it puts you to sleep!

2. Try Doodling

Bypassing your rational mind for a few moments may be all you need to get creative ideas from another part of your mind. Stop "thinking" and relax. Don't force any ideas. Just let your pencil or pen do what it wants.

Do any new ideas come into your mind as you doodle? Afterward, look at your doodle with a totally open mind. Does anything about it (shape? texture? overall feeling?) suggest any possible new approaches for your writing?

3. Try Drawing, Diagramming, or Mapping

Think about your seed idea (example: *The Castles of Great Britain*). Then draw whatever picture comes to mind (example: *a tower*). Or devise a diagram (example: *a floorplan of a castle*) or a map (example: *plot of a castle grounds—castle, moat, garden*).

Does this visual approach suggest any new ideas for your paper?

Name: _____

Taking Advantage of Incubation Time

Ideas to Think About

Your Mind Keeps Working, Even When You Stop

Just because you have stopped working, this doesn't mean that your mind has! Do the preliminary work of programming your mind to work on solving a problem. Then you may need to relax—take a break—for the solution to come to you.

The fine art of letting things sit is called "incubation time." Incubation has resulted in some of the most important discoveries in history. It can help you with your research papers, too.

Know When It's Time to Take a Break

For all writers, there comes a time in the writing process when they know they are not working efficiently. One time when this commonly happens is in the early idea-generating stage.

This could be interpreted as a block, but it may not be. It could just be a signal from your creative mind that you are fatigued and should stop.

Make Use of Incubation Time

Don't work harder than the task requires. If you have put in enough programming time and nothing's coming, maybe it's time to take a break. Trust that your mind is still working, even when you give yourself a break.

But be ready to catch ideas when your mind is ready to give them to you.

Techniques to Try

1. Know When It's Time to Take a Break

Don't keep working when it's time to stop. Listen to your inner self. Get to know how your mind and body signal you when you've reached your limit.

2. Be Ready to Record Fresh Ideas When They Occur

Once you've given ideas time to incubate, make sure you're ready to record them when your mind is ready to communicate with you again. You never know when the solution to your problem may arise—while you're taking a shower, doing home chores, even while you're sleeping. So carry a small notebook in your pocket. Keep a pencil and paper by your bed. Just be ready!

3. To Make Best Use of Incubation Time, Get Started Early

Getting an *early* start on any writing project makes it possible for you to make the best use of incubation time. By insuring enough time in your work schedule to allow for incubation breaks, you can make use of your creative brain at its *fullest* capacities.

Name: _____

Working Out a Preliminary Plan for Your Paper

Ideas to Think About

Why It's Helpful to Have a Plan

You've generated and developed some starting ideas about possible approaches to your paper. What next?

Before you move on to research, you need to have at least a *preliminary* idea of how your paper could be organized. The research phase of your writing assignment will be much easier if you go into it with a tentative idea for organizing the paper.

Do Your Ideas Suggest a Controlling Idea for Your Paper?

Review all the preliminary ideas that you have generated. Do they all seem to point to or spring from one important central idea?

Does Your Assignment Suggest a Specific Shape for Your Ideas?

Your assignment is another possible source of guidance in how to organize your ideas. Often your assignment asks you to include specific kinds of information in your paper or to answer specific questions that suggest ways to plan your attack.

Techniques to Try

1. **Consider Possible Structures for Your Paper**

    a. **What Patterns Do Your Own Preliminary Ideas Suggest?**

    Spread out all your ideas in front of you. When you look at all the ideas you've generated, does any particular pattern suggest itself?

    Do your ideas fall easily into subgroups of ideas? Do those subgroups suggest an overall structure for the paper?

    b. **What Patterns Does Your Assignment Suggest?**

    Look carefully at your assignment. Does it suggest or imply a possible focus or structure for organizing the ideas you have generated?

    Does it ask you to focus on specific questions? Does it suggest possible ways to break up the structure into separate parts?

2. **Make a Rough Plan**

    Once you have considered various possible approaches, try to settle on the one that seems most promising. You may find it helpful to write out your plan in a rough description.

    Draft a short paragraph (in complete sentences) that includes the following two starter phrases:

    - "The Main Idea of My Paper Might Be . . ."
    - "I Could Break Up My Paper into the Following Sections . . ."

3. **Remember to Stay Flexible**

    Of course, at the same time that you are making a preliminary plan for your paper, you must remind yourself to stay flexible. You will want to be able to adjust your plan as you discover new information or get new ideas about how to structure your paper even more effectively.

Name: _____

Writer's Block V: Getting Bogged Down in Research

Ideas to Think About

Don't Turn Research into a Chore

Because research requires you to collect information from a range of different sources, it can seem very confusing. What information do you need? Where will you find it? It's easy to get lost and discouraged.

Focus Your Search with a "Questions Map"

It's common to let yourself get sidetracked in the research stage. So make a plan to guide your research *before* you start. What *specific* questions do you want answered in your research phase?

A "Questions Map" can help to keep you on track and prevent you from getting overwhelmed by the wealth of information you may encounter.

Don't Let Research Turn into a Bore—Keep Yourself Interested

If you have taken the time to focus on a topic that really interests you, the detective work that research requires won't seem as much of a chore. Remind yourself of the reasons why you chose this topic in the first place, and keep your curiosity alive!

Let your research take you in new and surprising directions. What can you learn that you didn't know when you first started your project?

Techniques to Try

1. **Make a "Questions Map" to Focus Your Search**

    Prepare a "Questions Map" to help you center on the information you want to find:

    a. First, review your preliminary plan. Make a list of the key questions that your research paper should answer.

    b. Then, review this list of key questions. What other more focused questions do they suggest?

    c. Finally, add any other questions to your list that specifically interest you. What personal questions about your subject would *you* like answered—whether the information ends up in your final paper or not?

2. **Keep Your Interest in the Research Topic Alive**

    Keep your curiosity alive while engaged in research.

    a. Focus on what *new* information you are learning. How does it change how you view the whole topic?

    b. Keep looking at your topic from new perspectives. Do different sources look at your topic from different points of view? Does this suggest new approaches to your topic?

    c. Don't give up your own point of view. When you come across new information, ask yourself, "Where do *I* stand? How does this information compare with what *I* believe?"

3. **Take Time Out During the Research Process**

    Overwork in the research stage can make you stale and fatigued. Make sure to schedule enough time in the research stage so that you can take periodic breaks away from it to renew your energies.

Name: _____

EXPLORING AVAILABLE RESOURCES

Ideas to Think About

Where Do You Start?

A major task of a research paper is to assemble information about a specific topic from a *variety* of sources. The library looks so big, it's hard to know where to start.

What Reference Materials Are Available to You?

Research papers often draw on a range of source materials which can include:

- Books
- Periodicals
- Newspapers
- Encyclopedias and other reference materials

Review with your teacher or librarian what sources are available to you in your school and community.

What Kinds of Sources Will You Need for Your Project?

Different projects require different sources. For example, a history research paper might primarily rely on books dealing with historical subjects, while a paper dealing with current events issues might draw more on contemporary magazine or newspaper articles.

Techniques to Try

1. **What Kinds of Resources Are Best for Your Paper?**

    For your paper's needs, which kinds of sources seem most likely to be a good source of information? What kinds of reference materials does your assignment ask you to consult?

2. **Review How to Make Use of *All* the Research Tools of Your Library**

    You can make your task much easier if you make sure at the start that you fully understand what library resources are available and how to find them.

    The Card Catalog. Do you know how to use the title, author, and subject headings of a library card catalog to find possible book sources for your paper?

    Periodical Guides. Do you know how to use the library's periodical guides indexes? They will help you locate articles in magazines that are related to your research topic.

    Newspaper Indexes. Do you know how to use the library's newspaper indexes to locate newspaper articles that might pertain to your project?

    The Librarian. One of the librarian's most important tasks is to help library users find the materials they need. Don't be afraid to ask for help.

© 1991 J. Weston Walch, Publisher

Name: _____

PREVIEWING SOURCES BEFORE PLUNGING IN

Ideas to Think About

Don't Rush into Reading the First Reference Material You Find

It's tempting to jump right in, carefully taking notes from the first source you find that seems to apply to your topic. But this can turn out to be a tremendous waste of time.

Ultimately you will save yourself time by evaluating the range of source materials available to you *before* beginning your in-depth research.

Take Time at the Start to Scout Out *All* Possible Sources

Only after making a quick overview of all available sources can you wisely choose which sources are best and seem worth investing the time to read more carefully.

Then Take Time to Preview the Most Promising Sources

You can learn a great deal about the contents of a research source without taking the time to read it carefully. By taking a few minutes to preview your most potential sources, you can save yourself hours of wasted effort and time.

Techniques to Try

1. **Make Yourself Aware of All Possible Sources**

   Have you investigated *all* sources of research materials that might be of help with your project?

   Have you made full use of the library research tools described on Sheet 24: the card catalog? periodical guides? newspaper indexes? the librarian?

2. **A Method for Previewing a Potential Research Source**

   Every potential source—whether a book, or an article in a magazine or a newspaper, or an encyclopedia article—offers many quick clues about whether it will be a helpful source for your paper:

   Title. Does the title suggest that the content and approach of the book or article fit *your* research needs?

   Date of Publication. Is the source up to date or dated?

   Table of Contents (or Paragraph Headings). Do the chapter titles or article headings suggest how much the source might apply to your paper topic?

   Index. Does the index contain listings of topics that will be included in your paper?

   Illustrations and Captions. Does the source include illustrative material that offers clues about its contents?

   Opening and Closing Chapters (or Paragraphs in an Article). Does the opening and closing material indicate the author's main objectives? Does it provide any clue about the author's biases toward the subject? How does this approach relate to your paper's needs?

© 1991 J. Weston Walch, Publisher

Name: _____

SOME IMPORTANT TIPS ON NOTE-TAKING

Ideas to Think About

Set Up a Note-Taking System—and Stick to It!

Research for a research paper requires you to keep track of a lot of detail. You *have* to keep yourself organized, so decide on a system that will work for you—and use it.

A Plug for the Note Card System of Note-Taking

Students use many different ways to take notes for their research. Recording notes on note cards is one highly recommended method that allows you easily to keep track of the source for each piece of information you record.

Using note cards also encourages you to record information in small, isolated units that are easy to shuffle when it comes time to organize your ideas before you write your first draft.

Some Tips About Using Note Cards

One Note Per Card. Recording just one piece of information on each card forces you to concentrate on just the essential information you need. You record information in a way that makes it easy to organize later.

Summarize. Concentrate on not writing more than is needed to record the necessary information.

Take Notes in Your Own Words. Record key ideas in your own words. Only record word-for-word items you think you may wish to include as direct quotations in your final draft.

Abbreviate. Don't write whole words when you can abbreviate. Make up your own abbreviation shortcuts to substitute for names or ideas that recur in your research.

Techniques to Try

Suggestions for Setting Up a Note Card

Each note card should include the following items:

Source Information. Make certain you have carefully recorded *all* the source information you will need when preparing your paper's bibliography: the *author* and *title* of the work, the *city of publication,* the *publisher,* and the *date of publication.* You should also include the *library call number* of the work so that you can find it again easily if you need to.

To save effort, you may choose to record the specifics for each source on a separate bibliography list. Then you can mark each note card with just a code word abbreviation.

Page Number. It is very important that you record the exact page number(s) in the source where your information is found. You may need this information in order to go back to the source later on, and you will *definitely* need it if you cite this source in footnotes or endnotes.

Category Code. If you have already organized your paper into sections, you might also want to mark each card with a category code to show which section it belongs in. Category codes will be very helpful when you begin to sort your cards in the organization stage that follows your research.

© 1991 J. Weston Walch, Publisher   *Term Papers Step by Step*

Name: _____

Understanding and Avoiding Plagiarism

Ideas to Think About

Plagiarism Is a Serious Offense

Plagiarism is defined as using another writer's words or ideas without crediting the source.

Plagiarism is considered a serious offense in all schools. Students are responsible for understanding which source materials need to be cited and how to cite them properly.

What Material Needs to be Cited?

1. **Direct Quotations.** Any time you quote exact words from another source, you must include that material in quotation marks and cite its source.

2. **Paraphrases of Another's Ideas.** Even if you restate another writer's ideas in your own words, you must still cite the source of the ideas.

3. **Facts or Statistics That Are Not Common Knowledge.** Any fact or statistic that is not considered to be common knowledge should be cited. But information that is readily available in many sources—such as historical dates, or general biographical information about famous figures—does *not* need to be cited. For example, Martin Luther King's birth date is common knowledge and *would not* need to be cited. But the source of a specific fact about his early life that would not appear in most accounts of his life *would* need to be cited.

Techniques to Try

1. **Strategies for Avoiding Plagiarism**

    Follow these strategies to avoid plagiarism problems in your writing:

    - Put quotation marks around *ALL* material that you copy verbatim when taking notes.

    - When you are *not* quoting an author's words exactly, avoid paraphrasing the ideas too closely. Make certain to summarize the idea entirely *in your own words* to avoid accusations of plagiarism.

    - Keep track of all *ideas* that need to be cited:
      1) any idea that is not your own; and
      2) all facts, statistics, and other information that would not be considered common knowledge.

2. **Study How Other Writers Follow the Rules of Citation**

    You can learn a great deal about standard citation practices by studying how references are handled in the research materials that you read for your paper. Can you figure out why each author has chosen to cite the material in the way he or she has chosen?

3. **Get Help *Before* You Run into Trouble**

    If you still have questions about avoiding plagiarism, make sure to talk to your teacher before submitting your final paper.

© 1991 J. Weston Walch, Publisher

Name: _____

LOOKING AHEAD TO YOUR PAPER'S FOOTNOTES OR ENDNOTES

Ideas to Think About

Why Do Research Papers Require Footnotes or Endnotes?

Citations of your sources appear as footnotes if they appear at the bottom of each page, or as endnotes if they are listed at the end of your paper.

Such citations are included to credit sources that you have consulted in preparing your paper. They also allow your readers to consult any of your sources that may be of special interest to them.

Citation Notes Don't Have to Be a Big Deal

Don't make following citation form into more of a chore than it needs to be. Once you are clear about what material needs to be cited, all you need to learn is the accepted forms to acknowledge your citations correctly.

Prepare Ahead—Record Source Data While Doing Your Research

Citing sources is easiest if you get yourself into the habit of carefully recording all the citation information you need *while taking notes*. If you have to go back to get information, it will take extra time, and someone else may have already taken the source out of the library.

Techniques to Try

1. Ask Your Teacher What Note Style to Follow

Citation styles can differ depending on the course for which you're writing your research paper. Ask your teacher what style format you should follow and what other specific format may be required.

2. Sample Footnotes in the MLA Style

The following examples follow the style of the Modern Language Association, a format used in many humanity disciplines. These examples suggest models for a few of the most commonly encountered citation situations.

a. First Citation of Source in Notes

- *Single Book, Single Author*
  Author's Full Name, *Book Title* (City of Publication: Name of Publisher, Year of Publication), page number(s).

- *Single Book, Two or More Authors*
  Authors' Full Names [*], *Book Title* (City of Publication: Name of Publisher, Year of Publication), page number(s).
  [* Listed in the order that their names appear on the title page]

- *Essay or Article in Anthology*
  Author's Name, "Title of Article," in *Book Title*, ed. Full Name of Editor(s), Edition # (City of Publication: Name of Publisher, Year of Publication), page number(s).

- *Article in Newspaper, Magazine, or Other Periodical*
  Author's Name, "Title of Article," *Title of Publication*, Date of Issue, page number(s).

b. Shortened Citations of a Source Cited Previously in Paper

Author's Last Name, page number(s).

Name: _____

LOOKING AHEAD TO YOUR PAPER'S BIBLIOGRAPHY

Ideas to Think About

Why Do Research Papers Require a Bibliography?

Just as for footnotes or endnotes, the purpose of including a bibliography is to credit sources that you have used in preparing your paper. A bibliographic list at the end of your paper also allows readers to follow up specific sources of interest.

What Sources Should You List in a Bibliography?

All bibliographies include a full listing of every source that has been cited in the paper's footnotes or endnotes.

Some bibliographies, often labeled "Works Consulted," also include sources that were used during the research stage but were not included in footnote or endnote citations.

Record Bibliography Source Information While Doing Your Research

Just as with footnote and endnote citations, you should get into the habit of carefully recording *all* the bibliographic information you will need while taking notes.

If you prepare a careful source list *in exact bibliographic form* while you do your research, then all you will need to do later when drafting your paper is to alphabetize it to complete your bibliography!

Techniques to Try

1. Ask Your Teacher About What Bibliography Style to Use

Confirm with your teacher how extensive a bibliography you are expected to prepare. Should your bibliography just list sources that are cited in your footnotes or endnotes? Or are you also expected to include works that you consulted but did not cite?

2. Sample Bibliography Citations in the MLA Style

Like the examples on Sheet 28, these samples follow the Modern Language Association style. In general, bibliography citations contain the same information as their related footnotes or endnotes. But be sure to notice where bibliography style *differs in format*.

Single Book, Single Author
Author's Last Name, Author's First Name and Initial. *Book Title*. City of Publication: Name of Publisher, Year of Publication.

Single Book, Two or More Authors
[In alphabetical order:] First Author Name [*last* name first, as above], Remaining Author Names [*first* names first, as in note style]. *Book Title*. City of Publication: Name of Publisher, Year of Publication.

Essay or Article in Anthology
Author's Full Name [*last* name first]. "Title of Article." In *Book Title*. Ed. Full Name of Editor(s) [*first* name(s) first]. City of Publication: Name of Publisher, Year of Publication.

Article in Newspaper, Magazine, or Other Periodical
Author's Full Name [*last* name first]. "Title of Article." *Title of Publication*, Date of Publication, page number(s).

Name: _____

WRITER'S BLOCK VI: TRYING TO AVOID MAKING AN OUTLINE

Ideas to Think About

Planning Your Argument Is One of the Most Important Steps

Every research paper is constructed around an "argument"—the framework of key ideas that gives your paper its logical structure.

Students often skip over the important step of planning out the argument of their paper. They plunge into writing the first draft believing that they can save time by eliminating the "extra" step of outlining.

Why You Need to Plan Out Your Argument *Ahead*

Many students mistakenly attempt to organize their thoughts *while* they write the first draft. But the process of turning your thoughts into sentences is hard enough without having to worry at the same time about how those thoughts and sentences should fit together.

Without planning, the odds are that you'll end up with a first draft that lacks any clear organization and will need to be heavily rewritten! Making an outline *before* drafting will help you rehearse exactly what it is you want to say and point up problems at the idea stage where it's much less time-consuming to fix them.

Making an Outline Is Not as Difficult as You Think

Many student writers suffer from outline phobia. Just mention the word *outline* and they groan in despair. But organizing your ideas doesn't have to be a painful ordeal.

Like other complicated stages of the writing process, the important thing with making an outline is working at it step by step. The sheets that follow will show you how.

Techniques to Try

1. Do *You* Take Time to Outline Before Writing?

Take a moment to think about what process you have used to organize your ideas in past writing projects. Do you normally take time to outline ideas before writing your draft?

If not, do you run into any organizational problems later on? Could some of those be avoided by earlier planning?

If you do outline your ideas, do you still run into difficulties with organization in the drafting stage? Are there ways you might improve your outlining process?

2. What Makes Outlining So Difficult?

Do you suffer from outline phobia? If so, take a minute to make a list of the factors that make writing outlines so painful for you.

Share your list with other members of your class. What common problems do you share?

Name: _____

DETERMINING THE MAIN IDEA OF YOUR ARGUMENT

Ideas to Think About

A Well-Argued Paper Stems from *One* Main Idea

The main idea of your paper is the central point of your argument. It is the overall idea that your entire paper is trying to prove.

Writing textbooks refer to this main idea by many different names, including "thesis," "controlling idea," or "central premise."

The Importance of Determining Your Main Idea Early

Settling on a workable main idea for your paper as early as possible will greatly help you shape your material. Once you settle on the central idea of your argument—the main point you're attempting to prove—then the rest of your organization tasks fall right in line.

Working to Discover the Best Main Idea for Your Paper

You've completed your research and now you're faced with a huge pile of research notes. To make matters worse, your ideas have changed a great deal since you made that preliminary plan for your paper before starting your research. How do you determine the *best* main idea of your paper?

Unfortunately, the best choice may not always be obvious. It may take some work trying out different ways of looking at the material you have collected.

Techniques to Try

1. **Can You Already State the Main Idea of Your Paper?**

   Look at your early planning and research notes. Perhaps they already suggest a main idea for your paper.

   Try to phrase your tentative main idea in a *single* complete sentence. Work toward an "umbrella" sentence that covers the *entire* scope of your paper. (Example: *In his short career as president of the United States, Abraham Lincoln proved his greatness both as a skilled politician and as a devoted humanitarian.*)

2. **Still Stuck? Try These Methods for Finding Your Main Idea**

   After working on your research for some time now, you have more ideas about your paper than you think. Try some of these approaches to discover your main idea:

   Organize Your Notes into Groups. Quickly sort your ideas into the first logical groupings that occur to you. When you're finished, ask yourself, "What central idea unites them?" If no solution comes to mind at first, try another set of groupings.

   Freewriting. Use freewriting (see Sheet 17) to develop a rough paragraph of a tentative introduction for your paper. On a clean sheet of paper, write: *"In my paper, the main point that I wish to discuss/argue is . . ."*

   Clustering. (Review Sheet 18.) Choose your best seed word as the center of a cluster. Do any of your branches seem best to express the main point of your paper? Recluster if necessary.

   Talking Out Your Ideas with a Receptive Listener. Sometimes explaining your ideas to someone else is the best way to discover what you really have to say.

Name: _____

Developing Your Argument with Subarguments

Ideas to Think About

Your Main Idea Needs to Be Supported by Subarguments

Once you've determined at least a tentative main idea for your argument, you need to break up your overall argument into a small number of powerful subarguments to group the ideas of your paper in a balanced framework.

Subarguments Should Be Parallel

Many students work to develop subarguments to support their thesis, but their subarguments appear scattered and don't really seem to belong together. For example:

> **Main thesis:** **Dogs make the best pets.**
> **Subargument 1:** Cats are less good-natured than dogs.
> **Subargument 2:** Our family's dog, Buff, is a good watchdog.
> **Subargument 3:** It's good for lonely people to have pets.

Subargument statements should be phrased so they are parallel—all of similar groupings—and work together *in balance* to develop your argument:

> **Main thesis:** **Dogs make the best pets.**
> **Subargument 1:** *Dogs* are good-natured.
> **Subargument 2:** *Dogs* can act as good watchdogs.
> **Subargument 3:** *Dogs* make good companions for lonely people.

Arrange Your Subarguments in the Most Effective Sequence

Some subarguments will be more important to your thesis—or more interesting to your reader—than others. The order in which you present them has a definite psychological impact.

There is no definite solution, but many writers choose to:

1. Present their arguments in ascending order of importance, with the most important argument presented last.

2. Present an interesting argument first that will be certain to catch the reader's attention.

Techniques to Try

1. Developing Statements for Your Subarguments

Once you have determined a main idea for your paper, sort your research notes into the categories that naturally occur to you. Put to the side all material that does not seem to fit into one of your category piles.

Label each pile with a heading that expresses its main idea. Do the piles suggest possible parallel subarguments for your paper? If so, are there any important ideas in your discard pile that need to be included? Can they be worked in by changing the label on any pile to include them? If not, can you discover a revised way to break up your piles?

2. Write Out a "Sentence Skeleton" of Your Argument

Write your main statement on the top of a blank sheet of paper. Then write your subarguments below it *in complete sentences* in the order that seems best to you.

- Do all subargument ideas relate to your main idea?
- Are your subargument ideas expressed in parallel phrasings?
- Are your subargument ideas arranged in the best sequence?

Name: _____

CHOOSING THE BEST STRUCTURE FOR YOUR ARGUMENT

Ideas to Think About

There Is Usually More Than One Way to Organize the Same Material

Even after you are basically clear about the main idea and subarguments of your paper, you often still have choices to make as to how to present them most effectively.

For example, the very same research topic (example: *Patterns of Education in 19th-Century America*) can be organized in very different structures:

Chronological. You could describe the successive changes in educational practices that occurred during the time period.

Classification. You could group the different educational practices into different categories to discuss them.

Compare and Contrast. You could arrange the different approaches to education into opposing groups and then compare them.

Cause and Effect. You could analyze the overall problems of education in the 19th century and then show how different approaches attempted to solve them.

Experiment with Different Structures Before You Start to Draft

It's much easier to experiment with structures at the planning stage than later when you are writing your draft. You can change strategies in the idea stage with a lot less effort than later on when you have written a whole draft that you discover is not working.

Techniques to Try

Which Structure Fits Your Paper's Needs Best?

Different arguments make use of different structures. Which structure in the list above fits your material best?

Chronological. Does your paper lend itself to being organized by time sequence?

Classification. Does your paper lend itself to grouping its ideas into categories for discussion?

Compare and Contrast. Does your paper lend itself to comparing and contrasting two groups of opposing ideas?

Cause and Effect. Does your paper lend itself to analyzing the effects of one event, idea, or person on others?

Name: _____

SUPPORTING YOUR ARGUMENT WITH EVIDENCE

Ideas to Think About

The Function of Evidence

Your choices of a main idea, subarguments, and structure for your paper have provided you with a workable skeleton outline of your paper's argument.

Now it's time to begin choosing the specific evidence you will use to back up your claims. Evidence provides the meat to flesh out the bones of your argument.

Kinds of Evidence

You can draw on many kinds of evidence from your research to support the claims of your paper:

Facts	Quotations
Statistics	Graphs, Maps, etc.

Remember, however, that most evidence does not speak for itself. When you move on to writing your draft, you will need to do the work of interpreting your evidence for your reader and showing *how* it specifically supports your argument.

Don't Overuse Evidence

After immersing yourself in the research stage of your paper, it's tempting to want to include *all* your evidence in your final paper. But such overkill can often result in a cluttered paper.

Don't pack your paragraphs with evidence—select only the best evidence to support each of your ideas.

Techniques to Try

Considering Evidence for Your Argument

How do you decide which evidence from your research materials is strongest for your argument?

a. Consider each of your subargument statements. What major points will you need to convince your reader of? Where will you *need* evidence? How much will you need?

b. Now look at your research materials. What evidence do you have to choose from to support each point? Which piece of evidence would be most persuasive in convincing your reader?

c. Do you need to do more research in any area to find more effective evidence to support your ideas?

Name: _____

ANTICIPATING COUNTERARGUMENTS

Ideas to Think About

What Is a Counterargument?

A counterargument is any argument that a reader could use to argue *against* any claim made in your paper.

For example, suppose your paper argues strongly that the American Revolution was caused by British tyranny over the Colonists. A counterargument might claim that the *real* cause was, in fact, the Colonists' rebellious revolutionary spirit.

Anticipate Possible Counterarguments in Your Own Argument

In order to write your most persuasive argument, you need to anticipate counterarguments that your readers could think of to undermine the validity of your position.

One of the best strategies is to answer your readers' possible counterarguments in the text of your own argument—*before* your reader has a chance to question your thinking.

Avoid Counterarguments by Not Overstating Your Own Case

Remember, too, that in order for your argument to be persuasive, it has to be *reasonable*.

Be careful how you phrase the claims you make for your position. In your eagerness to defend your point of view, be sure not to undermine the persuasiveness of your argument by overstating your position or by making unreasonable claims that could be easily argued against.

Techniques to Try

1. Think Like Your "Opposition"

Now that you have put together a skeleton of your entire argument, put yourself in the position of an "opponent." Can you find any holes in your argument that need plugging?

a. Look for significant counterarguments that might be leveled against any of your subargument statements.

b. Anticipate possible objections against the evidence you have chosen to support your ideas.

c. Then, find ways to make yourself less vulnerable to attack:

- Can you change the way you have phrased your subarguments to make them more reasonable?
- Can you find stronger evidence to back up your claims?

d. Also anticipate ways that you might answer possible counterarguments in the text of your paper when you move on to drafting your argument.

2. Use Qualifiers to Avoid Overstating Your Claims

One important way to avoid making unreasonable assertions in your argument is by choosing carefully how you phrase your claims. Avoid *overstating* your case: Use qualifiers to make certain your reader doesn't think you are making a stronger claim than you mean to. These are just a few of the possible qualifiers to use:

Perhaps it *might* be agreed that . . .

It *could* be *suggested* that . . .

Isn't it *possible* that . . .

Although at first it might *seem* that . . .

Name: _____

Writer's Block VII: Struggling with Perfectionism

Ideas to Think About

Perfectionism—the Writer's Curse

"Perfectionism" for writers means not being able to keep a flexible attitude toward writing. Writers can become stuck revising the same words over and over, unwilling to move on until a section is perfect.

How Does Perfectionism Show Up at the Drafting Stage?

Perfectionism can be a particular problem in the drafting stage—when you begin to turn your ideas into full sentences:

- You keep starting over and are unable to keep a flow going.
- You hesitate to move on to the next sentence (or paragraph) until you feel your writing is polished.
- You keep checking back to earlier parts of your draft and rewriting to make sure these parts are good enough.

- You become overconcerned with little details (spelling, punctuation, how it sounds) rather than with the overall flow of your argument.
- Your anxiety leads you to procrastinate and delay getting started until the last possible minute.

What Causes Perfectionism in Writers?

Much perfectionist behavior results from unrealistic attitudes or ideas about how good writing is achieved:

- You mistakenly believe that writing should come out perfect the first time.
- You have learned at an earlier age that making a mistake or producing a messy paper is bad.
- You have unrealistic expectations about how good your own writing should be, or how easily it should be achieved.

Techniques to Try

1. Recognize When Your Writing Is Suffering from Perfectionism

Which of the perfectionist symptoms above fit *your* writing habits? Check them off. Do you recognize other writing behaviors in yourself and others that might be caused by perfectionism? Add them to the list.

2. Recognize Perfectionist Attitudes or Feelings

Which of the perfectionist attitudes or ideas described above fit *your* writing personality? Check them off. Do you recognize other attitudes in yourself or other writers that might also be classified as perfectionist? Add them to the list.

Name: _____

SOME IMPORTANT TIPS ABOUT WRITING THE FIRST DRAFT

Ideas to Think About

Fight Perfectionism—Don't Stop to Polish

The main purpose of your first draft is to add flesh to the skeleton of your argument. Get writing and keep moving! It's a waste of time to polish material that you may actually edit out of later drafts.

Stay in Touch with How You're Feeling

Don't let yourself automatically give in to perfectionist behaviors. Listen to your feelings and be ready to handle anxious feelings with healthy strategies.

For example, recognize when you're no longer writing efficiently. Take breaks *before* frustration builds to unmanageable levels.

Work on Maintaining a Flexible Attitude

Overcoming perfectionism may not be easy. It takes practice and effort to train yourself out of ingrained patterns and attitudes. Keep your sense of humor, and work to stay relaxed.

Techniques to Try

1. **Write a Fast and Sloppy First Draft**

   Don't sweat the small stuff now! Work fast to get a flow going, and keep writing.

   Don't stop to check spelling, grammar, or proper punctuation. Don't worry about how your draft looks on the page. Don't take time to read your words aloud to hear how they sound.

2. **Warm Up on the Easy Sections to Build Momentum**

   You don't *have* to write your draft in order. Warm up on the easy stuff before tackling the rough spots.

   For example, if the introduction is the most difficult part of your draft to write, start writing at a spot where you feel more confident. Then go back to your introduction.

3. **Recognize When You Start to Feel Uptight**

   Don't give in to perfectionist behaviors. Listen to your feelings. When you begin to feel anxious, try one of these tension-busting strategies:

   Break the Rules! Take control of your writing by playfully breaking the rules. (Example: *Write messily, with lots of scratch-outs; purposely misspell words; avoid punctuation altogether or make up your own.*)

   Try Freewriting. At the top of a blank paper, start writing about all your thoughts and feelings. Start each new sentence with the words "Now I . . ." (Example: *Now I am thinking that this paper is really going nowhere. Now I am thinking that I'll never finish this on time. Now I am . . .*)

   Lighten the Load. Alternate your writing chores with fun activities to keep up your spirits. (Example: *For every 45 minutes of writing, give yourself 15 minutes off to read a favorite magazine, write a letter, eat a snack.*)

© 1991 J. Weston Walch, Publisher

Name: _____

TACKLING THE INTRODUCTION

Ideas to Think About

Why Are Introductions So Hard to Write?

In an introduction, you want to summarize the essence of your paper in a short space and make it sound interesting to your reader. It's no wonder that many writers think composing the introduction is one of the most difficult tasks in any writing project.

What Elements Make Up a Good Introduction?

Every effective introduction shares these characteristics:

1. **It Clearly States the Main Idea of Your Paper.** To insure clarity, make sure to avoid cluttering the introduction with too many ideas. Save background material and detailed ideas for the body of the paper.

2. **It Outlines How Your Paper Will Be Organized.** Your introduction should give the reader a clear idea of the major points of your argument. Be sure to present these points in the same order that you present them in the body of the paper.

3. **It Excites Your Reader's Interest.** Your introduction should also present its ideas in such a way as to make the reader *want* to read your whole paper. One strategy is to start off with an interesting anecdote, quotation, fact, or statistic as an attention-grabber.

Study Introduction Strategies Used by Experienced Writers

All writers struggle with the challenge of writing effective introductions. Be aware in the magazines, newspapers, and books you read how other writers solve the introduction problem. What strategies do they use to make their introductions lively to interest their readers?

Techniques to Try

1. **Don't Try to Write a Perfect Introduction Right Off**

   Writing the first draft of a good introduction is especially hard because it comes first—before you're warmed up or know exactly what you want to say.

   Don't waste time in your first draft trying to write a polished introduction. More than likely, your ideas will change, or at least become more focused, as you complete the draft.

2. **Blocked? Try This Freewriting Technique**

   To help get your draft started, use the following freewriting model to compose a rough opening paragraph. Fill in each gap (ellipsis) with a sentence or two to explain the ideas of your paper:

   "The main idea I want to get across is . . ."

   "I will support my argument with the following points—in this order . . ."

   "My paper should interest the reader because . . ."

3. **Steal from Your First Draft's Conclusion**

   By the time you get to writing the conclusion of your first draft, you usually have a better feel for what you are writing about than you did when you started on the introduction. Often you can lift some of the final sentences of your first draft conclusion for your introduction!

© 1991 J. Weston Walch, Publisher   Term Papers Step by Step

Name: _____

Building a Strong Conclusion

Ideas to Think About

A Strong Conclusion Is Worth the Effort

Last impressions make a difference. A powerful finish leaves your reader with a satisfying impression of your argument. A weak conclusion, on the other hand, can seriously undermine even a good paper.

What Elements Make Up a Strong Conclusion?

Every effective conclusion shares these elements:

1. **It Clearly Restates the Main Argument of Your Paper.** To make certain your main idea has been communicated clearly, leave your reader with a concise restatement of the main idea of your argument.

2. **It Summarizes the Main Steps of Your Argument.** Remind your reader of the main points of your argument. Review the steps you have taken to support your main idea.

3. **It Contains Some Element That Is New.** A truly effective conclusion contains *more* than a summary of your paper's ideas. It leaves your reader with something new to think about—an appropriate closing quotation, a proposed solution for questions raised in your paper, suggested directions for further study.

Study Conclusion Strategies Used by Experienced Writers

Just as with introductions, you can learn a great deal by studying how more experienced writers solve the conclusion problem. What strategies do they use to summarize their arguments clearly and powerfully? What new material do they introduce to keep their readers' interest?

Techniques to Try

1. **Paraphrase When Summarizing the Key Elements of Your Argument**

   Try to avoid repeating earlier ideas word for word when you restate them in your conclusion.

   For example, look back to how you phrased the main idea of your paper in your introduction. (Example: *This paper will show that the Great Depression that followed the crash of 1929 was in many ways a healthy and necessary step in the growth of our nation's economy.*) To avoid repetition, can you think of a *new* way to express the idea in your conclusion? (Example: *In summary, many arguments suggest that the economy of the United States actually benefited from the crisis of the Great Depression.*)

2. **Strategies for Including *More* Than a Summary of Your Ideas**

   Since a strong conclusion goes beyond summarizing your paper's ideas, what strategies could you use?

   - **End with a Quotation.** Can you find a quotation from an authoritative source that eloquently sums up your position and/or places your topic in a wider context?

   - **Suggest Questions for Further Study.** Could the problem benefit from studies of parallel situations? (Example: *Study depressions in foreign countries to understand the U.S. Depression.*)

   - **Offer a Proposed Solution.** If your paper has analyzed the key elements in a problem (example: *the effects of single-parent homes on children*), end by suggesting a tentative solution.

Name: _____

DRAFTING PARAGRAPHS WITH PUNCH

Ideas to Think About

Strong Paragraphs Are the Building Blocks of Your Argument

Clearly focused and organized paragraphs are the building blocks of every well-written research paper.

Like the overall argument itself, each paragraph must be carefully constructed to support logically and express clearly its ideas.

Effective Paragraphs Focus on Only *One* Major Idea

Don't overload your paragraphs. Packed paragraphs tend to confuse readers if they try to present too many ideas.

Keep your argument easy to follow by restricting each paragraph to presenting just one major idea.

Effective Paragraphs Are Clearly Organized

Just as your paper needs to present a logical organization of ideas, so too do your paragraphs.

The Topic Sentence states the main idea of the paragraph (just as the thesis statement expresses the central idea for your whole paper). It often, but not always, appears as the first sentence of the paragraph.

Supporting Sentences fill out the remainder of the paragraph with material that expands on the topic sentence idea.

Techniques to Try

1. Test Your Paragraphs for Focus

Use the questions below to test whether each paragraph of your paper has a clear **focus**.

- Can you state the main idea of each paragraph in one sentence?
- Is that idea clearly expressed in an easily recognizable topic sentence in the paragraph?

2. Test Your Paragraphs for Organization

Use the questions below to test whether each paragraph of your paper is **well organized**.

- Does each paragraph offer sufficient evidence, in evidence sentences, to support its topic sentence idea?
- In each paragraph, does each evidence sentence clearly and logically relate to its topic sentence idea? Does any paragraph contain material that does not truly fit within the organization of the paragraph?

Name: _____

COMMUNICATING YOUR ARGUMENT WITH CLEAR TRANSITIONS

Ideas to Think About

Why Are Transitions Important?

Your readers need help following the logical flow of your paper. Strong transitions clearly communicate the structure of your argument. They act as signposts to your reader to mark when you are moving on to another point.

The Two Kinds of Transitions in Your Paper

Major Transitions mark the larger divisions between the major sections of your argument.

Minor Transitions mark the smaller divisions *within* each section of your argument.

Transitions Show Logical Connections Between Sections

All transitions, whether major or minor, show the reader how your ideas are logically connected:

Transitions Can Indicate a Series. (Example: *First, . . . Second, . . . Third . . .*)

Transitions Can Show Contrast with the Preceding Section. (Example: *Unlike* A, B *believes . . .*)

Transitions Show Cause and Effect Between Sections. (Example: *As a result of* X's attitude as described above, Y *was forced to . . .*)

Techniques to Try

1. Use Parallel Transitions to Make Your Structure Clear

You can help your reader to see your argument at a glance by wording your transitions, major and minor, in parallel phrasing to show how elements are related. (Example: *To* early observers, *the cause of the rebellion was ascribed to . . .* Writers of the next century, *however, believed . . .* Today, scholars *agree . . .*)

2. Strengthen the Major Transitions in Your Draft

Read through your draft and mark all the *major* transitions with a star.

Does each major transition clearly indicate to the reader that you are making a transition? Does it suggest a logical connection to the preceding section? Is each major transition phrased in parallel with other major transitions?

3. Strengthen the Minor Points of Transition in Your Draft

Read through your draft and mark all the *minor* transitions with a check mark.

Is each minor transition clear? Does it suggest a logical connection to the preceding section? Is each minor transition phrased in parallel with other minor transitions within this section?

Name: _____

Some Important Tips About Revising

Ideas to Think About

The Nitty-Gritty Details of Revising *Do* Matter

It may seem petty to you, but the final stages of revising often make the ultimate difference between a successful or an unsuccessful paper.

By presenting your hard-won ideas in their best dress, you make sure all your thoughts get communicated to the reader. If you don't take time to polish, you may be unable to appreciate all the hard work that you have done.

Plan Ahead for Revising Time

Time is the biggest problem most students face with revising. They don't save time to give the project the final polishing it needs and deserves.

Don't sabotage all the hard work that has come before. Budget time for revising and make sure you stick to your schedule.

Approach Revising Step By Step

Many students avoid the final stage of revising because they do not know exactly how to go about it.

You can make editing seem less overwhelming if you approach it step by step.

Techniques to Try

1. **Learn Editing Skills from Your Own Past Papers**

   You may want to forget past papers—especially if they were returned with lots of teacher's corrections. But your own papers are a *valuable* source of feedback about editing errors you have made in the past.

   Teacher's corrections often include specific ideas about how to correct such errors, too. Swallow your pride. What can you learn from your past mistakes?

2. **Make a Step-By-Step Editing Plan**

   It's important not to try to tackle everything all at once.

   a. First, slowly read your draft out loud. Don't stop to fix anything the first time through. What issues strike your attention? What's good? What needs work?

   b. Then use the sheets that follow to work through your revising process, step by step.

3. **Be Patient. . . . Revising Skills Take Time to Master**

   Like all writing skills, revising skills take time and effort to acquire. Be patient with your progress. For many students, polishing skills are the most difficult to achieve.

   Set specific editing goals to work on for each paper.

© 1991 J. Weston Walch, Publisher

Name: _____

DOUBLE-CHECKING YOUR ORGANIZATION

Ideas to Think About

The Organization of Your Draft May Still Need Clarifying

One of the most common teacher comments on research papers is "I have problems following the organization of your ideas."

You may have started off with a clear outline earlier in the process. But you can still end up with a draft containing organizational problems.

Does Your Draft Follow Your Original Organization Plan?

One problem arises when your argument plan changes while you are drafting your paper. Sometimes the best-laid plans can get lost in the process of drafting.

During the drafting stage, it's easy to lose your train of argument. It's also common to include new ideas while drafting, even if they don't actually fit into your original plan.

Can Your Reader Follow the Organization of Your Draft?

Another problem arises in the difficulty all writers face in trying to communicate ideas to their readers. Even if you think your argument is perfectly clear, that doesn't matter if the reader cannot follow your ideas.

One of the hardest tasks to master in the editing stage is to learn to read your work objectively, as if you were a reader seeing the material for the first time.

Techniques to Try

1. **Read Through Your Paper as Others Will Read It**

   All writers must learn to hear their own words as others will hear them. As you read through your draft, ask yourself:

   - Have I clearly communicated my main idea?
   - Do all my ideas relate directly to my main idea?
   - Have I presented my argument logically? Have I used clear transitions to lead my reader through my argument?
   - Are my paragraphs clear and focused?

2. **Use the After-the-Fact Outline to Check Your Organization**

   If you are still unsure about your draft's organization, try the "after-the-fact" outline as a double-check:

   a. Read through your draft, a paragraph at a time. Make a separate list, in note form, of all the key ideas in each paragraph. For example:
      PARAGRAPH #1:
      –Abraham Lincoln's early law career
      –Lincoln's family life
      –Pro-slavery attitudes in the South

   b. After completing an inventory of ideas in each paragraph, look over this master plan of your paper.

   c. Look within each paragraph list. Does the organization of each paragraph seem clear? Do any ideas not seem really to belong in the groups in which they appear?

   d. Next, compare paragraph lists. Do you see any repetition of ideas that might be combined or eliminated?

   e. How about the overall order of ideas throughout the outline? Do any ideas seem to be out of sequence? Is the order logical?

Name: _____

CHECKLIST FOR AVOIDING COMMON ARGUMENT FALLACIES

Ideas to Think About

What Is an Argument Fallacy?

A fallacy involves a specific violation of logic in the way an argument is constructed. In the interests of trying to present a persuasive argument, it's easy for writers to fall into various common fallacy traps.

The fallacies presented below describe some of the most common errors of argument found in student research papers.

Fallacy #1: *Sweeping Generalizations*

Sometimes in trying to construct a tight argument, you can fall into the trap of overstating or exaggerating a claim. One common way to fall into a faulty generalization is by making a broad statement based on too small a sample of evidence. (Example: *All students in the United States today believe that success in life is defined by making a large income.*)

Solutions

1. Check the phrasing of all general statements in your paper. Do you ever overstate the case? Have you supported your claims with sufficient evidence?
2. Use extreme care with all-inclusive words such as *all, every,* and *always*. Use qualifying words such as *some* and *sometimes* to temper your claims.

Fallacy #2: *Oversimplified Conclusions*

It's also easy to fall into the trap of reducing complex situations to oversimplified either/or solutions or oversimplified stereotypes. (Example: *Citizens who aren't willing to go to war for their country obviously don't know what it means to love their country.*)

Solutions

1. Beware of oversimplifying complex situations with either/or thinking.
2. Work to recognize and eliminate stereotypes in your thinking and writing.

Fallacy #3: *Poorly Defined Terms*

The logical validity of any argument depends strongly on the clarity of its terms. It's easy to use terms in your paper too loosely, overlooking the possibility that they may have *one* meaning for you but possibly *other* meanings for your reader. (Example: *Freedom . . . Justice . . . Morality.*)

Solutions

1. Define carefully all terms that play a major role in your argument. (Example: *In this paper I shall define "democracy" as any political system whose citizens freely vote for their leaders in elections with several candidates.*)
2. Especially be aware of abstract words. Make their meanings clear.

Techniques to Try

Check for Argument Fallacies in Your Argument

Read over the examples of fallacies above to familiarize yourself with common research paper fallacies. Then carefully read through your draft to look for and correct any fallacies in your argument.

Name: _____

Checklist for Eliminating Word Clutter

Ideas to Think About

Approach Self-Editing Step by Step

All writers, no matter how experienced, suffer from the problem of word clutter. It's impossible to write a first draft that doesn't need streamlining. Use the suggestions below to tackle the problem of word clutter in *your* writing.

Edit for Economy

One important goal of self-editing is learning to express your ideas in the *least* number of words.

Eliminate Unnecessary Words.
- Cut unnecessary adjectives (example: *the **global** international situation* = *the international situation*).
- Cut unnecessary adverbs (example: *The situation was **really** serious* = *The situation was serious*).
- Cut unnecessary prepositions and articles (example: *some **of the** participants* = *some participants*).

Eliminate Unnecessary Repetition. Read each sentence carefully. (Example: *All the teenage girls who were interviewed liked the new school gymnasium, and **all the teenage** boys **who were interviewed also liked the new school gymnasium**.*) Cut unneeded repeated words. (Example: *All the teenagers interviewed liked the new school gymnasium.*)

Simplify Over-Long Sentences. (Example: *The **process of** education has **become increasingly** more costly in many **of the** cities **of the** United States.* = *The cost of education has risen in many U.S. cities.*)

Turn Passive Writing into Active Writing

Another important self-editing goal is working to eliminate passive writing and to express your ideas as directly as possible.

Use the Active Voice. Replace passive verb constructions (example: *The ball **was hit** by John*) with active verbs (example: *John **hit** the ball*).

Avoid the Verb "To Be." (Example: *John Steinbeck **is** a great writer.*) Substitute a more explicit verb. (Example: *John Steinbeck used vivid characters and description to capture the taste and feel of the West like no other American novelist*).

Techniques to Try

Edit Your Draft by Reading Your Writing Aloud

It may make you feel foolish, but reading your own words aloud is by far the *best* technique for editing your own work. When you read your own work aloud, you hear problems that you tend not to pick up on when you just read silently to yourself.

Name: _____

CHECKLIST FOR DEVELOPING A MORE FORCEFUL STYLE

Ideas to Think About

What Makes a Writing Style Forceful?

Besides eliminating the problem of word clutter, you can develop other self-editing skills to enhance the readability and power of how you express your thoughts. Use the checklist below to edit your draft for a more forceful writing style.

Edit for Word Power

Working to expand your vocabulary is a very helpful way to improve the power of your writing style. But you don't have to sound like a walking thesaurus to write with style! Often the most powerful words are everyday words used simply and effectively.

Choose the Simplest Word for the Job. Don't strain to use a grand-sounding word (example: *commence . . . facilitate . . . utilize*) when a simpler one will do the job just as well (example: *begin . . . help . . . use*).

Choose Concrete over Abstract Words. Add power to your writing by using *specific* words wherever possible. (Example: **Several** abandoned **vehicles** blocked the **highway**. = **One** abandoned *1968 Volkswagen Bug* and *one 1958 Chevy truck* blocked **Route 66**.)

Be Attentive to Tone. Many words that seem to have the same denotation (literal meaning) have quite different meanings because of their connotations (emotional association). (Example: *Elizabeth I was a shrewd* **monarch** vs. *Elizabeth I was a shrewd* **queen**.)

Refining Your Sentence Style

Besides editing their writing for clarity, effective writers also edit their work to be pleasing to their reader's ear.

Vary Sentence Length. Too many long or short sentences in a row can be monotonous for your reader. Work for a balance.

Use Parallel Constructions. Don't mix different sentence constructions in the same list. (Example: *She liked* **to play golf** *and* **swimming** = *She liked* **playing golf** *and* **swimming** or *She liked* **to play golf** *and* **to swim**.)

Use Sound Effects. Skillful writers often make careful use of the sounds of their words to increase the impact of their sentences on their readers. One common technique is the use of alliteration, which links the first consonant sounds of a string of words. (Example: *Charlie Chaplin certainly deserves the title "Super Star of the Silent Screen."*)

Techniques to Try

Learn by Studying Other Writers' Styles

One of the best ways to improve your own writing style is to study the styles of other more accomplished writers.

Choose authors whose styles you admire. Read their work aloud. What kinds of words do they use to express their ideas? What qualities of their sentence style would you like to incorporate in *your* writing?

Name: _____

CHECKLIST FOR ELIMINATING SEXIST LANGUAGE

Ideas to Think About

What Is Sexist Language? Why Is It Bad?

Sexist language is language that stereotypes females and males according to traditional sex roles. Our culture's growing insistence on equality between the sexes has made today's readers particularly sensitive to hidden gender biases in the English language. When possible, modern writers try to avoid using sexist language.

Problem #1: *Recognizing Sexist General Nouns*

Many words have implied sex biases. For example, the word *man* or *mankind* is often meant to include both males and females: *Early societies of **man** lived as hunter-gatherers.*

Solutions

1. Substitute a nonsexist term: **humans** for **man**.
2. Rephrase: ***Our** first societies,* or *Early primitive **peoples**.*

Problem #2: *Recognizing Sexist Singular Pronouns*

Traditional English often uses singular male pronouns (*he, his, him*) to refer to both sexes: *Ask the corporate executive of the 80's—**he** will tell you about the importance of good grooming.*

Solutions

1. Use the double pronoun: **he or she** for **he**.
2. Change the singular noun and pronoun to plurals: **executives** . . . **they**.
3. Rephrase to delete the need for the pronoun: *When asked, corporate executives will tell you . . .*

Problem #3: *Look Out for Sexist Bias in Titles*

Many titles and generic terms incorporate hidden biases. These mask a gender bias that does not conform to the reality of today's world: *The chair**man** of the committee called the meeting to order.*

Solutions

1. Substitute a nonsexist title: **chairperson** instead of **chairman**.
2. Use a more specific title: **senator** or **representative** instead of **congressman**.

Techniques to Try

Be Creative

Sometimes the English language offers no easy alternatives to problems of sexist language. You have to choose the best of all available solutions—and sometimes make up your own.

Be aware of how other more experienced writers tackle the difficulty of eliminating sexist language from their writing.

Name: _____

Checklist for Avoiding the Most Common Grammar Errors

Ideas to Think About

Don't Let Grammar Get You into a Panic!

It's easy to feel that you will never be able to master all the rules of grammar! Like all effective learning, the important thing is to work at it step by step. The sections below explain two of the most common problem areas: "illegal" sentence construction and faulty verb tense.

The Sentence Fragment and the Comma Splice

The sentence fragment is an incomplete sentence punctuated as if it were a complete sentence. (Example: *George Washington was the first U.S. president. **And the greatest one.***) Eliminate fragments by combining them with "legal" sentences. (Example: *George Washington was the first, and greatest, U.S. president.*) Or turn fragments into complete sentences. (Example: *He was also the greatest one.*)

The comma splice incorrectly uses a comma to join two independent clauses together. (Example: *Joan of Arc was branded a witch**,** she was burned at the stake.*) There are three ways to correct a comma splice:

1. Use a **period** to break up the clauses into two sentences. (Example: *Joan of Arc was branded a witch**.** She was burned at the stake.*)
2. Use a **semicolon** to make the clauses into one complete sentence. (Example: *Joan of Arc was branded a witch**;** she was burned at the stake.*)
3. Use a **comma and conjunction** to make the clauses into one sentence. (Example: *Joan of Arc was branded a witch**, and** she was burned at the stake.*)

Verb Tense

When to Use the Present and the Past Tense. Use the **past** tense to report actual historical events. (Example: *Napoleon **spent** the remainder of his life imprisoned on the island of St. Helena.*) But use the **present** tense to discuss plot events in literature. (Example: *When Romeo first **appears** in Shakespeare's* Romeo and Juliet, *he **believes** he **is** deeply in love with a girl other than Juliet.*)

Techniques to Try

Get a Good, Readable Grammar Book to Answer Other Questions

To help master your grammar and punctuation questions, ask your teacher or librarian to recommend a suitable reference book that you will find easy to use—so that you will actually use it!

Name: _____

Checklist for Avoiding the Most Common Punctuation Errors

Ideas to Think About

Don't Let Punctuation Be a Problem in Your Writing

With a little work you can conquer punctuation problems in your writing. Begin by mastering the punctuation rules in the following list.

Commas

Use to Separate Items in a List. Common usage now recommends putting a comma before the final conjunction (*and, or*) in a list. (Example: *The basket displayed apples, oranges, and peaches.*)

Use Following an Introductory Clause or Phrase. (Example: *After the queen recovered from her illness, her subjects showered her with presents.*)

Use Before Coordinating Conjunctions (*and, or, but*). (Example: *The freezing point of water is 32 degrees, but the freezing point of mercury is much lower.*) If the clauses being connected by the conjunction are very short, however, the comma can be omitted. (Example: *It rained and it snowed.*)

Semicolons

Use to Separate Two Short Clauses in a Sentence. (Example: *John ran to the store; Mary rode her bicycle.*)

Use to Clarify Complex Lists that Include Commas. (Example: *The time capsule contained a box of historic photographs; a red, white, and blue quilt; and a typewritten greeting from the mayor.*)

Colons

Use to Introduce Lists. (Example: *Carlos dreamed about his favorite foods: cheeseburgers, french fries, and ginger ale.*) However, the clause before the colon should be able to stand as a complete sentence. (Example: *My favorite foods are:* is not correct.)

Use to Introduce Indented Quotations. Long quotations (four lines or more) or lines of poetry should be introduced by a colon and indented, single-spaced in the body of your paper.

Techniques to Try

Make a Grammar and Punctuation Checklist of Your Past Mistakes

Make improving your grammar and punctuation a long-term goal for your writing. Keep an ongoing list of the kinds of grammar and punctuation errors that you have made on past papers—as well as examples of how to correct each error.

Name: _____

Writer's Block VIII: Skipping the Final Step—Proofreading

Ideas to Think About

Make Time for the Final Step: Proofreading

A paper full of surface errors communicates a message. It says that the writer just didn't care enough to go the extra mile. An otherwise powerful paper that is full of misspellings and typographical errors leaves a bad impression on the reader—and often receives a lowered grade.

Don't Give Up at the Finish Line!

Yes, you're sick of the whole project. You've stared at these same words for weeks. It's tempting to throw in the towel. Don't!

Do be aware, however, that your tired state of mind may not put you in the best proofreading frame of mind. Be *extra* diligent as you look at your work for the last time. Because you are so familiar with your own words, you are likely to miss errors that a fresher reader (your teacher) may pick up easily.

What Kinds of Errors to Proofread For

These are some of the common proofreading errors to look for. You may want to read your paper over a few times to check for each category separately.

Spelling Errors

Typographical Errors

Words Omitted, Repeated, or Transposed

Lines Omitted, Repeated, or Transposed

Punctuation Marks Omitted

Paragraph Indentations Ignored

Computer Spacing Errors

The overall look of your final presentation also has an important impact on your reader. Try to keep erasure marks, page wrinkles, fingerprints, and similar eyesores to a minimum.

Techniques to Try

1. **Methods for Proofreading Your Own Work**

   Reading Aloud. Read your paper aloud slowly, line by line. Read the punctuation marks out loud as well as your words.

   Reading Backward. Read your paper backward, starting with the last word of the last paragraph. Reading backward helps you focus on the text word for word, rather than in context as when you read it sentence by sentence.

2. **If You Use a Computer Spellchecker**

   Be careful not to rely on your spellchecker for your last check. Spellchecker programs don't recognize nonspelling errors (dropped words, repeated words, etc.). They also don't flag correctly spelled words that have been misused (such as mixing up *to*, *two*, and *too*).

3. **Calling on Others to Proofread Your Work**

   In the final hour, a willing friend or family member can be a great help. But remember that the ultimate responsibility—and pride of achievement—is yours. Take time to give your work the last read-through, and take pride in a job well done!